A John Verney Collection

"We've left it up there because it
contains my husband's last breath."

By the same author

AUTOBIOGRAPHY
Going to the Wars (1955)
A Dinner of Herbs (1966)

FICTION
Every Advantage (1961)
Fine Day for a Picnic (1968)

FOR CHILDREN
Look at Houses (1959)
Friday's Tunnel (1959)
February's Road (1961)
ismo (1964)
The Mad King of Chichiboo (1963)
Seven Sunflower Seeds (1968)
Samson's Hoard (1973)

HUMOUR
Verney Abroad (1954)

ANNUALLY
The Dodo Pad (1965–)

A
JOHN VERNEY
COLLECTION

Introduction by Craig Brown

" *I got them with a right & left...* "

The Alastair Press

Published by
The Alastair Press
2 Hatter Street
Bury St Edmunds
Suffolk

First published in 1989

© John Verney 1989

ISBN 1 870567 51 X

"Your manuscript is both good and original;
but the part that is good is not original
and the part that is original is not good."

Typeset in 11/14 Bembo by
Rowland Phototypesetting Ltd
Printed in Great Britain by
St Edmundsbury Press Ltd, both of
Bury St Edmunds, Suffolk

Contents

"The Marquis of Granby speaking..."

Prelude

'Autobiographies are the rage at present,' she said. 'The wrinklies are all doing them. You should do yours, Grandpa.'

She didn't add 'before it's too late' but that's what she meant. In fact it's already too late. I used to enjoy writing, especially if I was allowed to illustrate what I wrote, but nowadays even a short thank-you letter has become a dreaded labour.

Still, my grand-daughter had set off a train of thought which, I felt, might be worth following. After the war I used to contribute light-hearted fragments of autobiography to various publications—Collins Magazine for Boys and Girls, the Cornhill, GO Travel Magazine, the Young Elizabethan, the National and English Review. . . . Presumably I still owned the copyright. If I could find some of them, and make appropriate acknowledgements, they would amount to an autobiography of sorts.

I consulted my friends Stephen and Alison du Sautoy of the enterprising Alastair Press. On reflection, they agreed to take the risk if I would include a selection of joke drawings from the Dodo-Pad, the annual Diary which I started in 1965 and which, published ever since by Collins in Glasgow, still has quite a large following of Dodopadlers. Their suggested title for the book was A John Verney Collection and—of far more importance to me—they said that Craig Brown was willing to write an Introduction. His brilliant articles in *The Times* and elsewhere have been a great source of pleasure to me and my wife in recent years.

When all the material was assembled I showed it to the same grand-daughter for comment. 'Um . . .' she said thoughtfully, with a glance at my wrinkled features and moth-eaten garments. 'Shouldn't the title really be A Collection FOR John Verney?'

John Verney
October 1989

Introduction

Every owner of a Dodo Pad, described in John Verney's Who's Who entry as 'the amusing telephone diary', will have pondered, at one time or another, over the true identity of the enigmatic Lord Dodo, the omniscient figure whose aphorisms and doodles, historical recreations, snippets of vital information, scenes from family life, advice, jokes and ribaldry festoon each and every page.

Writing this introduction on Friday 3rd November 1989, I only have to look back to yesterday to discover that on the 2nd November 1887, Sir Alfred Domett died. Who on earth was Sir Alfred Domett? Across the page, Lord Dodo fills us in. '"What's become of Waring, Since he gave us all the slip" wrote Browning. Waring was his friend the poet Alfred Domett—he'd become Prime Minister of New Zealand'. Tomorrow, Saturday, is, it seems, the anniversary of Berlioz's The Trojans, first performed in Paris in 1863. In celebration, Lord Dodo has drawn four grand Trojan soldiers marching across the top of the page, and, opposite, a large picture of two fierce Trojans fighting each other, one with a dodo discreetly emblazoned on his shield.

Sneaking a look ahead a fortnight, I chance upon a riddle. 'What things increase the more you contract them?' I don't know, so I have to turn two pages to 6th December. The answer is 'debts'. 6th December is St Nicholas's Day. St Nicholas, Lord Dodo informs us, 'saved three girls from prostitution by throwing three bags of gold into their window. He is also the patron saint of pawnbrokers and his emblem is three balls'. At the foot of the page, we learn that Paolo Uccello, who died on 10th December 1475 'is one of Lord Dodo's favourite painters . . . Vasari tells how he refused to continue work on a mural because the Abbot fed him on nothing but cheese'.

While all other diaries—Office diaries, Boy Scout Diaries,

Slimmers Diaries, Motorists Diaries—are small islands of dullness and relevance in an otherwise interesting world, the Dodo pad, compiled under the all-seeing eye of Lord Dodo, remains all the time alert, funny, dotty and marvellously, passionately, irrelevant. Lord Dodo may well be the patron saint not only of doodlers but of all day-dreamers everywhere.

Lord Dodo is, in fact, John Verney, and John Verney has many other guises too. He has written a sad and funny book of war memoirs, 'Going to the Wars', he has written children's books like 'Friday's Tunnel' and 'ismo' (which became something of a hippy cult on the American college circuit), he has written travel books and short stories and articles galore. And, throughout his seventy five years, it seems he has never stopped drawing and painting upon whatever surface has seemed most handy.

John Verney likes to wear a hat and he holds his cigarette at a jaunty angle. A red-and-white spotted hankie sprouts from his old tweed jacket. He smiles a lot and is full of stories. He welcomes you up to his studio in a loft with a cheery shout and the offer of a cigarette and a cup of coffee. Like John Verney himself, the studio is everything you would have hoped it would be: paintings and drawings and doodles and caricatures are scattered about the place in a sort of partially tamed higgledy-pigg勒diness. As he writes in this collection of his old drawings, 'to retain them lovingly is to some extent to defeat Time'.

He likes to paint furniture, and, as with everything he creates, it is always touched with his wit, and with his love. At the top of the stairs, the seat of a wooden chair has two hands painted upon it, ready to welcome the next sitter. At one end of the studio stands a pretty screen he has painted for his cousin, Bishop Stephen Verney. In the centre panel sits Florence Nightingale, whose sister married Sir Harry Verney, their great-grandfather. Next to the screen there is an old chest, painted for a friend who is having a bit of trouble with his neighbour. The neighbour, an uncouth sort of fellow, is depicted leaning over the wall with a pair of binoculars, peering into the friend's bedroom. All sorts of things seem to be happening in the rest of the neighbourhood, including a naked couple entwined under a blanket beneath a tree. Who might they be? 'Oh, just a couple who have tucked up there for the night' explains John Verney, with a twinkle in his eye.

His conversation swoops with ease and grace through his wide array of interests—from his childhood in India ('I remember snakes and mongooses and Kipling') to his days at Eton, through memories of Vienna in the Thirties to a recreation of dialogue from The Third Man, from the family he adores ('Have you met my daughter Rose, rather a marvellous girl actually. . . ?') to his new enthusiasm for the novels of David Lodge. In this collection, John Verney writes of Ardizzone's war drawings that, 'In their tender and satiric fashion, they reaffirmed human values and showed the comic spirit everywhere bursting through the bonds of uniform even in the midst of tragedy'. The same, I think, is true of Verney himself, for the amusement and delight recreated in his works is founded upon something very humane and very touching, something, like the Dodo Pad, to keep us smiling through the days gone by and through days to come. Wherever Sir Alfred Domett and St Nicholas and Paolo Uccello and Florence Nightingale and Berlioz and all those Trojans may have ended up, I am sure they are already jostling for key positions in the next Dodo Pad, and in the next Collection of the marvellous John Verney.

Craig Brown
Ridgewell, November 1989

s

"Sofari sogoodi..."

My Finest Hour

The theme is a supra-artistic concept. Pudovkin.

The late Charles Laughton and I once murdered a ginger tom-cat which belonged, I recall, to a Mrs de Groot. The strange fierce animal's meteoric exit from this world down a ventilator shaft at Elstree Studios haunts me still. And since Mrs de Groot must by now have gone the way, metaphorically speaking, of her cat, perhaps the story can safely be told.

The Studios had been built originally for silent films. Later, each hangar had been equipped with an inner soundproof shell, which left a high narrow space between it and the outer walls. These dimly lit corridors were like part of a German Expressionist film, and entering them at one end I often fancied I saw the distorted shape of Dr Caligari himself disappear round the other. At each corner a large open ventilator, 10 ft above the floor, sucked out the stale air with a faint whirr.

The film, called *St Martin's Lane*, was about a kind old busker, Charlie (Charles Laughton), who befriends a beautiful street dancer, Libby (Vivien Leigh); then her talent is spotted and she jumps to stardom, kicking poor old Charlie into the gutter as she takes off. There were five assistant directors. But since the first two did all the work necessary, a menacing fog of boredom hung over the heads of the remaining three. The third filled his time flirting with Vivien Leigh. The fourth got an occasional break booking the Director's table for supper at the Savoy or, the next morning, fetching him bismuth tablets. I was the fifth.

Naturally I was not so naïve as to suppose that the star-producer would recognise in me the hope of British films when, aloof with god-like preoccupation, he floated down on to the set and off again. Sometimes, if I was quick enough, I opened the door or unfolded his canvas chair, marked with large letters on the back 'Mr Laughton'. But my talent could not be expected to shine through these simple acts, though it tried hard. No, my hope lay rather with the Director. I was full of good ideas for improving the script; and, since I had nothing else to do, I kept at his elbow waiting to share them with him, if he asked. He didn't ask. A nervous dyspeptic, whose stomach too evidently was much on his mind, he remained throughout noticeably unaware of the presence, not to mention the potentialities, of his Fifth Assistant, though he did once refer to me, out of my hearing, as 'that over-educated page-boy'.

The remark reached me through my friend Julian, the Third Assistant, a tall dark laconic young man who played Satie on the property piano in the lunch break and who first introduced me to Proust. Julian had already been some years in the industry, so could smile at my enthusiasm. 'If you want to be a Director,' he used to say, 'you had better start by forgetting that "the theme is a supra-artistic concept" and concentrate instead on beating the Fourth Assistant to the bottle of bismuth tablets.'

I concentrated rather, for interminable hours and days, on criticising the pathetic lack of imagination with which the Director placed his camera. Somehow or other, no one in the Oxford Film Society had told me that angle shots went out of fashion with cloche hats.

But my chance came.

The day began very much like any other, with a 5 a.m. alarm bell in my bed-sitter off the Cromwell Road; a walk through streets still lamplit to the South Kensington Underground; an hour's train journey into daylight and the Hertfordshire suburbs, via Golders Green and the second volume of the *Guermantes Way*. Waiting to be checked in, I noted the ginger tom-cat curled up, as usual, in the warmth of the gate-keeper's office. As usual, I handed him a fragment of the ham sandwich I carried in my pocket for lunch. In the past four weeks the gesture had become one of those comforting superstitious rituals, like not walking on the joins of the pavement, with which I daily propitiated the forces of providence and in which, who could tell, lay a surer magic to promotion than that afforded by the Director's bismuth bottle. Hitherto the tom-cat had invariably sneered at my offering. This morning he accepted the ham greedily. It was a portent.

There was only one scene to be shot this particular morning, after which we packed up and moved into London for a long sequence in the Drury Lane Theatre, hired for the purpose. It was quite a simple shot, opening with the distant view of St Paul's at first light. Then the camera's eye, floating somewhere in the upper air above Covent Garden, would move in on a cat squatting in the gutter outside Charlie's attic window. The window would open and Charlie, wiping the sleep from his eyes, would say 'Hullo pussy' and let her in.

The cat played no part in the story. The object of the scene was to build Charlie up as a nice chap who was kind to cats and thus to win, on his behalf, the hearts of several million cat lovers.

We expected to have the shot in the bag by 11 a.m. A model was to be used for the distant view, the attic stood four feet above the studio floor, the cat had merely to edge a few inches along the gutter, miaow affectionately and enter the window. Even her line of dialogue could be dubbed in afterwards. Still, you can never be sure with cats and a special cat-man, with his team of acting cats, had been engaged at twenty-five guineas for the day. When I reached the studio he was already there, with two large baskets; a melancholy figure alone on the deserted set with the smell of plaster, paint and woodshavings.

The scene on the studio floor livened up in its habitual way. The chief cameraman gave directions about lighting; the First and Second Assistants paid a rush visit; Julian wandered in to tell me a story he had heard Vivien Leigh tell the evening before; the Director arrived, followed by the Fourth Assistant armed with a water jug and the bismuth bottle; and Charles Laughton himself, disguised as Charlie, came across from the dressing-room. At length we were ready to shoot and the cat-man selected the most precocious of his cats.

In the next hour or two all the acting cats were tried in turn, but not one of them on this occasion would act. Either they just squatted in the gutter, blinking foolishly at Charles Laughton, or they backed hurriedly away from him, to rejoin their master where he stood, biting his nails with vexation, outside the camera's range. The preamble to the shot was abandoned; all efforts were concentrated on simply shooting the cat entering the window of Charlie's attic. All efforts failed. The morning passed, the afternoon wore on. And still the shot stayed out of the bag. Technicians groaned, Charles Laughton rolled his eyes in despair, the Director alternately raved at the cat-man and swallowed bottlesful of bismuth. The First and Second Assistants telephoned every agency in town for other cat-men, but none were available. Julian hid saucers of sugared milk behind geranium plants on the window sill. The Fourth Assistant rubbed Charlie all over with cats' meat. But still not one of the cats would play the simple part, and their master grew frantic in his efforts to explain their unaccountable loss of talent.

It was about 4 p.m. when the Fifth Assistant remembered the ginger tom-cat and saw the opportunity he had so long waited for.

'Here, what are you doing with that cat?' the gate-keeper shouted.

I lied, breathlessly, that Mr Laughton himself wished to borrow the cat.

'Sorry, mate. You still can't have him. He belongs to an old lady across the road, Mrs de Groot. A foreign lady and very queer about cats. She'd skin me if she knew I'd let you take Tommy. You must go and ask her yourself.'

Argument, then bribery, proved useless and a few minutes later, carrying the ginger cat, I knocked on the door of a semi-detached villa, one of a row opposite the studio gates. While waited, two Cheshire cats grinned at me in the parlour window, then vanished as footsteps sounded in the hall. When the door opened the issuing smell of cats almost knocked me over. Mrs de Groot herself stood on the threshold. I had never seen anything like her before, nor have I since. She was about ninety-five, over six feet tall and dressed entirely in black lace except for a tiger skin hat. Dyed red hair hung around her wrinkled face. She clutched half a dozen cats in her arms, a further dozen crowded

about her ankles, peering up at me. The two Cheshire cats I had seen in the window crouched one on each shoulder.

'Ach, Tom-mee, there you are. Komm in,' she said to the cat I was holding. Apparently I didn't exist.

Tommy struggled, but I held on to him. Mrs de Groot looked me in the face, and for the first time I noticed her eyes. They were bright yellow with small, wedge-shaped pupils. I explained the purpose of my visit. She spoke and understood very little English, but enough to turn my request down angrily. I began to see what the gatekeeper had meant about her skinning him.

'But this cat is always at the studio gates,' I insisted desperately.' I could have taken him and brought him back and you would never have known.'

'Not known?' She stared at me as if I must be half-witted. 'Of course I know. Tom-mee tells me afterwards.'

I tried a different approach. With my free hand I pulled out my wallet. 'Naturally we would expect to pay you. . . .'

The monstrous old creature became kindlier. 'Ach, you pay. How moch?'

'A pound.'

'Feelm people reech. Two pounds.'

We settled for thirty bob, cash down. It was all I had in the world. And I swore that I would personally bring Tommy back again to her within half an hour. As I ran back to the studio I prayed that the shot in progress had been a flop like the rest. It had. No one was particularly hopeful that my amateur cat would succeed where the professionals had failed, but at this point in the ghastly day anything was worth trying. Only the cat-man protested something about Equity and his cats' professional reputation, but he was pushed aside and I took his place. I settled the tom in the gutter and, when the cameras turned, stepped back out of view. He stayed there quietly purring and the entire studio staff held its breath. Charlie opened the window.

'Hullo, pussy,' he murmured drowsily.

The tom stretched himself, walked a pace or two, miaowed, then jumped affectionately into Charle's arms. One could almost hear the exclamations of delight from millions of cat-lovers all over the world. The shot was 'in the bag' at last. The Director threw his hat in the air, the cameraman slapped the side of his camera, and the shout of general relief on the floor was echoed by the electricians high up among the arc lights on the gantry. And Charles Laughton, stroking the cat, turned to me and said 'Good boy.' It was my finest hour.

At that moment the ginger cat went mad. The noise, the lights being switched off, something or other frightened him. Crazed with sudden terror, he leapt out of Charles Laughton's arms and, screeching horribly, set off on a wild steeplechase round the studio, pursued frantically by the Fifth Assistant. For no one else gave a damn what happened to him. But then no one else had seen Mrs de Groot.

The door out of the studio into the corridor was normally kept closed, but now, by mischance, it had been opened. I saw the danger too late; the tom got there first. There was no way out of the corridor except through swing doors at one end, which were shut. I tried to block the course as he came past on his third circuit. He flashed between my legs like a furry thunderbolt.

Then, reaching the corner, the poor misguided creature spotted the ventilator. It was a hole, it spelt safety. At full speed he gave a prodigious leap and, with a despairing shriek, disappeared into it for ever.

I didn't see Mrs de Groot again. The gatekeeper sent a message that she was waiting for me at the entrance, carrying a large knife. I left the studios hidden under a rug in Julian's car, and never returned. Nor was there any particular sequel to the story of the cat, except, possibly, the disgusting smell, some weeks later, under the studio floor. But I only heard that from Julian long afterwards. For next day we started shooting the sequence in the Drury Lane theatre.

Perhaps it was this change of environment, perhaps just the basic ingratitude of film people in general, but my single contribution to the making of St Martin's Lane was instantly forgotten. In all the following weeks the Director never once asked my advice, never again did Charles Laughton turn to me and say 'Good boy.' I lost all interest in the picture; and, while scene after scene was shot, I spent the days hidden cosily from general view on the floor of the Royal Box. Partly I read Julian's copy of Within the Budding Grove, partly I slept. Ambition to become a Director slowly died, and when, at the end of the shooting, the Mayflower Picture Company paid me off, it was quite dead.

Some time after Munich the completed film of St Martin's Lane was shown to the public. I found that the scene with the cat had been cut, and I wasn't even mildly depressed. But I also found, unexpectedly, that I had left my mark on the picture, after all, in rather a different way. You may remember that wonderfully affecting scene at the end when Libby, now a world-famous star, runs across Charlie, still in the gutter, and how, eaten with sudden remorse, she takes him with her into Drury Lane, where she is due for a rehearsal. There Charlie realises his life's ambition by standing alone on the historic boards and declaiming 'The green eye of the little yellow god' to a sprinkling of cynical producers and impresarios, who, for Libby's sake, hide their yawns as politely as possible. And you may remember, too, how, on the sound track, Charlie's voice reciting the adventures of Mad Carew is accompanied by a gentle undertone of snoring. The critics hailed this effect afterwards as 'a brilliant stroke', 'the real Laughton touch'. As it happened, the effect was accidental. The snoring was mine.

Just tell them that I have found it impossible to discharge my duties as I would wish to do without the help & support of the woman I love!"

Here's that sick squid I owe you."

'The Black Death started under
the armpits and spread across Europe...'

"If we had some eggs we could have some
eggs & bacon — if we had some bacon..."

" I'm a little stiff from polo."
" I couldn't care less where you come from!"

"Death-watch beetle has been confirmed in the Choir."

Meeting Captain Ardizzone

'Isn't he the chap who did the one you showed me the other day?' the Brigadier said. 'Sort of bleeding roots of a tooth, only I was holding it upside down.'

'No, sir, that was a Graham Sutherland. Ardizzone does the ones of army life you did like.'

'Oh, those. Yes, I did like them. There was one of a Brigadier, obviously plastered as an owl and making a pass at a FANY. What I wish I was this minute.'

In the shelter of the ACV he and the Brigade Major wearily compiled the long casualty return. A coating of white dust on eyebrows and hair gave them the look of actors crudely disguised as octogenarians, and added to a general effect of exhaustion. Trickles of sand drifted through the roof and lodged in the nose, mouth and ears, making conversation tiresome—and a diplomatic handling of the matter essential. It was a measure of our affection for the Brigadier that, on his staff, we preferred him to do what we wanted of his own accord.

'I believe he's a rather good chap,' I went on casually. 'Amos says he was with the Rifle Brigade in that show on Kidney Ridge. We watched it going on our right, sir, if you remember.'

'Was he? Must have had a ticklish time. I'd like to hear about it. Why not ask Amos to bring him to dinner tonight?'

'I'll see if I can arrange it, sir,' I said, and caught an amused glance from the Brigade Major. 'You and your social life,' it seemed to say.

'Oh, by the way, Victor Bone's coming,' the Brigadier added. 'Ran into him at the Div. conference this morning. Poor old Victor, he has three tanks left. I thought he needed a change. Do us all good to have a bit of a party. Pity there's nothing to drink except whisky.'

'Well, actually, sir,' I said, '*actually* I have a little surprise. . . .'

There never seemed to be any women; and a little song was enough. So one was thrown back a good deal on wine. It's surprising how steadily it flowed, all things considered, from the beginning in Palestine where the early Zionists had thoughtfully made it their first task, to the bitter end in Rhineland when, in a manner of speaking, we trampled out the vintage where the grapes of wrath were stored. But in between came a long wineless period, the dearth only broken once, that I recall.

A show at the Leicester Galleries, the chapter in Monty's memoirs on Alamein, a Christmas present of some chianti, various chance things have revived the episode. Especially, I daresay, the chianti. . . . My little surprise was eight bottles of it—well, of something of the kind.

The advance had swept on, leaving us in a battered state near Mersa Matruh. Swanning about that afternoon I had spotted a store tent, sodden, collapsed and half-buried by sand, in a waste of rusted gerry cans, tank spares and barbed wire coils, the jetsam of an army rout; and had driven the jeep cautiously past the sign of a skull creaking in the icy wind. Peeled back, the canvas revealed a thousand packets of pumpernickel, a hundred round cheeses the size and consistency of cannon-balls, and the eight straw covered flasks, unmarked and unopened, a forlorn relic, symbol almost, of the German–Italian alliance.

At Div. HQ on the way home I called in to report how they might make themselves sick on cheese and pumpernickel, and to invite my friend Amos to dinner in the Brigade Mess.

'You know,' he said blandly, when I'd shown him the attraction, 'it really does look sometimes as if life may, after all, be guided by more than mere chance. Ardizzone—that war artist you're so keen on—has turned up out of the blue for the night. We've nothing much to offer here in the line of company or booze, and one gathers from his pictures that he likes both. Do you think your delightful Brigadier would mind?'

'It may be tricky,' I said. 'He's in bad form at present and doesn't want any guests till we've had a chance to organise the mess—you don't count as a guest. I'll send a DR back with the answer if I can fix it.'

It seemed very important to fix it. I had approached the ACV warily, and, the mission achieved, hastened to send the DR. After which, as there was nothing else to do, I lay down in a flea bag under cover of the jeep, to reflect pleasantly on the treat ahead.

In the spacious early days I carried everywhere whopping great tomes on the Impressionists, but with prolonged exile my thought turned more and more, from necessity as well as choice, to what was going on in that way back in England. The Impressionists, too bulky to lug around, were replaced by an ever-shifting stack of postcard reproductions and war-artist booklets in which the shapes of writhing girders, shattered façades and mummified tube-shelterers testified to the impact of the Blitz on sensitive and gifted men at home. Other pictures acquainted me, rotting wistfully in the Middle East, with the physiognomy of heroes high-lighted in chalk, with the patriotic efforts of male and female electric-welders, and so on. The artists of all these I greatly admired, some because they had been inspired by the war to their best work, others for their deadly competent draughtsmanship. But the experiences they transmuted, or embalmed, were not mine; nor did any of them seem much concerned with the predicament, as I knew it, of ordinary flesh and blood people rigged out in uncongenial clothes and torn between devotion to the common task and the demands of their natures. Were the welders always so worthy? Did no one back in England, in spite of the war, laugh and drink and make love any more?

With almost a shout of joyful recognition, therefore, had I first come on the work of Edward Ardizzone. Here at last was an artist—a man, too, I was to discover—who kept things firmly in their right perspective.

Primarily, of course, the drawings enchanted me with their pictorial skill; but beyond that, they portrayed the war world I lived in, of bored and ribald soldiery pretending to be Birnam Wood, of bibulous officers and listless sentries, of members, remote but manifestly feminine, of the QAIMNS. Possibly they were not a profound comment on war itself—at any rate I liked them the better for not aiming to be. But in their own tender and satiric fashion, they reaffirmed human values and showed the comic spirit everywhere bursting through the bonds of uniform, even in the midst of tragedy. In short, they pleased me no end.

So did the prospect of meeting their author, as I lay in the shelter of the jeep, that late afternoon in November on the Libyan shore.

'A bore about Victor Bone, though,' I thought. I could foresee difficulties there—as might a hostess who, having arranged a particularly *recherché* little dinner, is descended upon by her most uncouth relative. I was fond enough of the bewhiskered and bewhiskied old warrior. But when he got drunk—and there was no reason to suppose he wouldn't—he tended to be brusque, not to say insulting, with strangers who didn't hunt. I doubted if Edward Ardizzone hunted. Still, he was a soldier as well as an artist, he'd probably know the form. And I was turning over in my mind some of the things I looked forward to discussing with him, when the Brigade Major, passing by, prodded me in the ribs with his foot.

'I suppose this means we'll have to listen to you talking art all the evening,' he said.

He arrived with Amos just before dark, a blue-eyed jolly-faced Dickensian sort of man, English as the drawings from which he might have stepped. He was rather taller than I had expected, and rather thinner—he told us he'd lost many pounds with the Rifle Brigade—and seemed perfectly at home as a soldier; indeed a few long wisps of hair showing beneath the khaki beret with its GS badge were the only visible trace of a bohemian disposition resolutely sacrificed, I imagined, to the war effort.

I had little opportunity to talk to him myself, but I studied him closely—till the light failed—and had the impression of a gentle and tactful person who preferred to adapt himself to the company of the moment, but who, nevertheless, in any matter which affected him deeply, wouldn't budge an inch.

'We won't wait for Colonel Bone,' the Brigadier said to the mess sergeant; and to us, 'Old Victor never could read a map. Do you remember that exercise in Palestine. . . .'

The dust storm had changed to a clear desert night. Wearing hats and coats we sat out under stars, a happy crowd of about a dozen, most of whom had been long together. Captain Ardizzone obviously preferred to share our military gossip than talk art; was more interested in the chianti, perhaps, than in either.

'I say, what a splendid sight!' he exclaimed as the bottles were placed on the trestle tables.

I was glad to see, from where I chatted with Amos farther along, that the Brigadier and Brigade Major were delighted with our guest, going over experiences of the battle they had in common. The wine, too, played its part in the evening's success. Sour and stinking, all you could say was that, in the circumstances, it was better than nothing. I've drunk worse all the same in English hotels at 25s. the bottle.

'One understands how it got left behind,' Amos said. He and I found that a slice of cheese on pumpernickel effectively took the taste away. Captain Ardizzone drank his share; but sipping, where the rest of us quaffed.

The meal was half over when a tiny armoured car, known as a dingo, roared into the camp. A batman could be discerned unloading a valise off the back and Victor Bone swaggered towards us. A newly risen moon, I recollect, shed a romantic charm over his farouche and moustachioed form, and glinted on the hunting horn which as usual peeped from the breast pocket of his fleece-lined coat.

I noticed Captain Ardizzone stiffen, like a pointer; and could almost hear him jotting down a quick mental sketch.

'Sorry I'm late, Brigadier. I lost the way,' Victor Bone explained, wondering at the shout of laughter.

'Never mind, Victor. You look as if you've come armed to spend the night.'

'I have. "Where the MFH dines he sleeps. And where the MFH sleeps he breakfasts," you know. If that's all right.'

'Delighted. Take that place opposite. And have some of this stuff. Where's a glass?'

'Vino, by God. Trust the bloody Brigade HQ. . . .'

While a glass was fetched the Brigadier introduced him to

Captain Ardizzone across the table. Victor nodded coolly, his eye boggling a bit at the GS badge. He had no manners whatever; and of course was a military snob.

'Ha . . .' he said, knocking back the glassful. 'Damned good too, don't you think so, Ardy-whatsit?'

'Well, it's certainly very pleasant, up here in the desert, to be drinking anything which might remotely be called wine,' Captain Ardizzone politely agreed.

At length the party began to break up. The Brigadier retired to sleep, the Brigade Major took Amos off to the ACV on military business, and I made to seize the long-awaited chance of moving my place. But even as I got there Victor Bone's grotesque shape, swaying against the night sky, slumped down ahead of me. Baulked, I withdrew again to the shadow of the mess lorry.

'Oh, hallo, sir,' I heard Captain Ardizzone say.

The interest taken in artistic matters by officers, field rank and above, is a familiar, indeed welcome, phenomenon of the post-war era. But in 1942, in the best military circles, painting was still on a par with milk-drinking, so that the evening's success looked like being shattered when Victor started off: 'Someone said you're one of those war artist chaps.'

'Yes, I am actually,' Captain Ardizzone replied, in a defensive but still affable tone, waiting to see what next.

Victor was breathing heavily, his speech slurred, and I expected almost anything to come—except what came.

'Of course I don't know much about it myself, so I'd rather like to hear the opinion of a chap like you on this one. But it's always struck me that Lionel Edwards is the finest bloody artist of the lot. Would you agree?'

'I can't say I know much about hunting. He's certainly very clever.'

'Exactly. You've put your finger on it, Ardy Soany. Damn clever. There's one he did of us all out with the Mendip. You would recognise every horse and rider. Of course Cecil Aldin's possibly better at hounds. . . .'

For the next twenty minutes I listened, fascinated, to Victor working through the gamut of contemporary sporting artists of every type. Captain Ardizzone spoke little; occasionally assenting where he found it possible to assent, interpolating here and there a reference to Stubbs, Audubon and Leech as having set a standard by which such things should be judged. He seemed amused by the game. Certainly Victor was enjoying himself. Content that all was well, I left them discussing someone who does partridges under snow and went for a stroll.

When I returned Victor was saying 'Peter Scott now. There's another chap who can do it. I mean, those skies. *Exactly* what you get on the Wash.'

'Are they? Very dramatic skies, I'm sure.'

'Dramatic. Absolutely the word, Ardy Soany old boy. Marvellous the way he gets geese, don't you think?'

'I'm afraid I only know about geese on the table.'

'On the table. Ha ha. That's damn good. Like this vino. Let's open the last bottle. You know, I think this is the best wine I've ever drunk in my life.'

'I should imagine so,' Captain Ardizzone said. An unmistakable hint of restlessness had entered his voice.

Victor's taste in wine was quite unpredictable—the truth was that like most Yeomanry officers he had no palate whatever. But a certain expertise on the subject was part of the cavalry tradition and I had seen him hurl a perfectly harmless glass of port to the floor, calling it corked. Now, as the last bottle emptied, he began to enthuse about the stuff as if it was Chambertin. He had reached—I knew the signs—the aggressive-maudlin stage, when if you agreed with him you got a ferocious smack on the back; if you disagreed, the contents of a glass over your head, as likely as not.

By the light of the moon a wild and stubborn expression could be detected on Captain Ardizzone's otherwise cheerful countenance. I'd seen the same look, in the eye of an overloaded mule just before it kicked.

To my relief Amos arrived, to take his visitor home.

'Ardy Soany,' Victor was saying thickly. 'You don't hunt, but you're a good chap. So I'll tell you what this is. It's claret. . . .

Yes, claret . . . from Rommel's HQ . . . chianti bottles part of the cover plan.'

'Well, we'd better be going,' Amos said, and Captain Ardizzone rose.

Victor stayed put, holding his glass to the light. 'You're the sort of chap, Ardy Soany, who knows about wine. Come on now, what do you think it is?'

'Might be anything,' Captain Ardizzone said. 'But I would guess it was Italian boot polish.'

When I'd seen them off, I returned to finish what was left—for I had less palate even than Victor. He was still sitting there and looked at me morosely.

'That chap who was here just now,' he growled, 'know what he was? A bloody Eye-tie. In British uniform. And dining at Brigade HQ. Bloody scandal. . . .'

"My great-grandfather was killed at Waterloo."
"Which platform?"

"It's so sad about the poor Dean's physical disability."
"I never knew he had one."
"Oh yes. When I told him he ought to get married he sighed and said, 'I can never marry. I'm afraid my stipend is too small."

"According to this paper, ten thousand camels a year are used to make paint brushes!"
"It's amazing what they can train animals to do."

"And here we have the Megatherium which has been extinct for at least fifty million years."

"What do you think of euthanasia?"
"I prefer old age in Europe."

"I dreamt I came face to face with God last night."
"Oh really? What was He like?"
"Well, in the first place She was black..."

skoy-atto-lo

A terrible Celtic oath? The refrain of a Hebridean boat-song? No, merely the phonetic spelling of the Italian word for a squirrel—*scoiattolo*. It came into my life, or rather I came into its life, soon after I moved to my present abode, a cell converted into a studio in an ancient Florentine monastery.

It was in the bleak mid-winter, frosty wind made moan, earth stood hard as iron, water like a stone. But the Florentine climate is eccentric and, emerging from the side door of the cinema, we were caught in a rainstorm and had to dash for cover across the street into a pet shop. *We* consisted of myself, two friends called Mr Thesiger and Mr White who happened to be wintering in Florence, and Giulietta, a fourteen-year-old girl whose family occupied other converted cells in the monastery. I must say a word about Giulietta (pronounced by the way, Jooly-ate-her).

Basically there are only two classes of people in the world. Those who squeeze toothpaste out of a tube neatly and conscientiously from the bottom; and those, the vast majority, who seize the tube irresponsibly by the middle and leave it looking like a street accident. Giulietta is in the first class. She's the eldest of the family and is up long before dawn to get her sisters and herself washed and fed and ready for school. She works late into every night doing her homework and theirs. Between whiles she nurses a sick mother, manages a lazy good-for-nothing father and somehow finds time to look after a small menagerie of hamsters, budgies and other pets, besides feeding most of the stray dogs, cats and birds in the area. She is the sort of girl who lavishes more love on every little feathered or furry creature than even the most besotted mother would dream of giving a sick baby. We had taken her to *Mutiny on the Bounty* (in Italian) in order to give her a well-earned treat and because we wanted to see whether the new and much publicised version was an improvement on the film we had enjoyed thirty years before. Twice on the way to the cinema we had to restrain her from dashing suicidally across the street to stroke a kitten.

The pet shop proved to be full of budgerigars, canaries, rabbits, hamsters and mice. There was even a baby alligator in a tank. Mr White, above the sounds of twitterings and scratchings, told us how he had once trained a goshawk. Mr Thesiger described being attacked by a crocodile. I compared Trevor Howard and Marlon Brando with Charles Laughton and Clark Gable, greatly to the latter's advantage. But, though Giulietta speaks excellent English, her thoughts were not with us. Soon we realised that she was not with us either. We found her in the back of the shop, kneeling beside a little cage in an attitude of rapt devotion. The cage contained a young squirrel. Mr White and Mr Thesiger proclaimed it to be a red squirrel—not the grey tree-rat that has killed off the rest in England but the genuine Beatrix Potter kind, with tufted ears, a bushy tail, a white tummy and a white circle round each beady black eye. Not that its exact species troubled Giulietta. In its cramped cage, the poor thing was obviously miserable, terrified and half-starved. Occasionally it hurled itself against the bars, then crouched again in a corner, its whole body palpitating. Giulietta's nose was pressed against the cage while she uttered what were intended to be, and perhaps were, low comforting noises.

We stood watching her. Then Mr White said, 'Do you know, I shan't be able to sleep tonight unless I buy Giulietta that squirrel.' He reached for his wallet.

'I agree,' said Mr Thesiger, reaching for his. 'We'll go shares. I had a tame squirrel as a boy and it went everywhere in my pocket.'

'But where will Giulietta keep it?' I protested. 'Her parents already disapprove of her pets and in any case there is not a spare inch of space left in their flat.'

'She can keep it in your studio,' they said. 'The ideal place. Once it's been tamed it will be able to jump about on all those beams and bookcases and picture frames. . . .'

I glanced again at Giulietta. Her ears were pink and she was hardly breathing. So, with a deep sigh, I, too, reached for my wallet. . . .

That, of course, was only the beginning. The first problem was to provide a better cage for the squirrel while the taming process went on. The next morning I drove to see Angelino on the farm where I spent last year. I returned with the inside of my Fiat 500 filled with straw and with a dilapidated rabbit hutch tied on the roof. Then I bought a roll of close-mesh wire netting, a hammer, wire cutters and a kilo of staples. Then I went to the market and came back with bags of walnuts, almonds, Brazil nuts and indeed every other kind of nut obtainable in Florence. Then I found I'd forgotten nut-crackers. . . .

By the time Giulietta returned from school that evening, all was ready. Mr Thesiger and Mr White came too, to offer expert advice. We tacked the netting securely round the old hutch to make escape impossible, we improvised a door in the wire, we spread straw and placed tasty fragments of nut with as much care as if we had been preparing for a cocktail party. The next question was where the cage should be situated. The studio is lit by large French windows opening on to a balcony. Mr White, Mr Thesiger and Giulietta decided that, if I wouldn't mind moving my easel and paints away from the light, that would be the best place for the cage, so that the squirrel could enjoy a view out on to the hillside with olives. Beside the balcony is a huge ilex, its lower branches actually touching the window. They felt that this would complete the squirrel's illusion of a free country existence.

All that remained was to usher the squirrel into its new home—I say *it* because the question of its sex was never precisely established and remained a matter of dispute between Mr Thesiger and Mr White. So far it had remained all day quietly huddled in the little cage from the shop. But the minute we moved it into the large new cage it went mad—and not, I'm afraid, with joy. It hurled itself at the wire netting walls and roof, its tiny black claws clutching and releasing the mesh faster than the eye could follow. For nearly an hour it raced round and round, gnawing at the wire and wooden framework with its teeth, searching for a means of escape with such ferocity that we had hastily to reinforce the netting with a double thickness and many extra staples. Really, by the way it went on, we might have been tormenting it instead of bending over backwards in our efforts to be kind.

'Squirrels are like children,' I said, 'they don't appreciate all you try to do for them.'

'After all, why should we expect them to?' said Mr Thesiger.

Even Mr White was taken aback by the squirrel's lack of resemblance to Squirrel Nutkin. 'All depends on whether it was born in captivity, or captured wild,' he said to Giulietta. 'If the former, then I'm sure you will succeed in taming it. Otherwise, well. . . .'

However, the problem of taming it had to be postponed because the squirrel, after the first frantic hour, suddenly withdrew into the straw in an inaccessible corner of the cage and there hibernated for the next month.

I sleep in the studio. Every morning, before leaving for school, Giulietta would come in to crack a supply of nuts and change the water. 'Any signs in the night?' she would ask.

'Well, I think I heard it moving around at 2 a.m. and again at 4.30.'

'It seems to have eaten some of the walnuts but I think it may prefer almonds. Could you please get some more?'

'Oh, of course,' I said.

Every evening, when she got back from school, Giulietta would again rush into the studio to see if the squirrel had stirred during the day and crack a further supply of nuts for the night. It seldom had stirred but the nuts steadily vanished just the same. Instead of getting on with my work I found myself peeping furtively into the cage, making comforting noises. Mr Thesiger and Mr White were forever coming round to see how things were progressing. 'Any signs of life?' 'No, still mostly sleeping.' We began to worry that it might be ill, or even dead. We poked a stick into the straw, to uncover it, but the squirrel was very much alive, its black eyes shining at us from the dark recess, its flank heaving with fear. Once we helped Giulietta to reach in through the netting-door to stroke it, but that provoked the squirrel into another frantic fit of escape-mania, so we desisted.

But with March and the first signs of spring, matters improved. The squirrel, which by then seemed fully grown as far as I could judge, became less nervous and more adventurous. It now spent a large part of every night clambering about the cage, or cracking and chewing ever greater quantities of nuts. Sometimes, if I was awake, I switched my bedside light on to see what it was doing, but it always vanished quickly into the straw. It seemed more confident by day and often, as I worked away busily, I had the odd impression that it was quietly watching me. But it was still essentially wild and never allowed Giulietta to do more than stroke it with the tips of her fingers. If she tried to lift it in her hands it would cower back into the straw or else leap frantically around the cage.

With April, and the full tide of spring, the scene outside changed almost hourly. One day the peasants were ploughing with white oxen among the olives, the next they were sowing, and only a few days later, as it seemed, the earth was carpeted in palest green. All winter the ilex trees outside my window had been silent. Now the few birds to have survived the shooting season began to be heard in the branches. A nightingale, in particular, sang there both by day and night. I thought I detected a gleam of cunning in the squirrel's eyes when I found them watching me. Giulietta was confident that she was making progress. 'He almost let me lift him this morning,' she would say triumphantly, and with incurable optimism. Mr White and Mr Thesiger were sceptical. They were leaving Florence and, with much wisdom and gentleness, they tried to persuade Giulietta that the kindest thing would be to set the squirrel free. There was plenty of food outside, there were no grey tree-rats and few dangers of any kind. She had done her best, but a wild animal was, after all, a wild animal. . . .

Giulietta said nothing. But it was clear enough from her expression that by this stage she would part as dearly from the squirrel as from life itself. By then even I, a creature of habit, had grown so used to having it in my studio that I didn't wish to see it go. I could not willingly be separated from something that had so successfully disrupted my life and work for three months.

The night of April 30th was especially clear and warm. For the first time I slept with the French windows open and in the ilex tree the nightingale poured out its unending tremulous song. The squirrel seemed unusually active, too. The sound of it leaping about the cage or nibbling at nuts had so long been part of the background to my dreams that I paid little attention. Once I nearly turned on the light to see what it was up to, but I didn't. I was woken on the morning of May 1st by Giulietta shaking me to say that the cage was empty. How it managed to get out we shall never know because the netting was intact. There was not even a loose staple. May 1st was a public holiday, Giulietta did not have to go to school. She spent the day wandering in the fields around the perimeter of Florence. The loss of the squirrel created a vacuum in her heart that needed to be filled very quickly indeed. . . .

For the past two months my studio has gradually assimilated most of the contents of that pet shop. I leave for England next week. Most of the budgies, canaries, hamsters and rabbits have been found homes one way or another. But the alligator is no longer a baby. . . .

Défense de toucher

Fatima ,   Fatissima   &   Non e possibile

Tea at the Embassy

I have only once been to tea in a British Embassy. It is long ago now, almost a quarter of a century and the wound has healed. The letter arrived by special messenger in a gold-crested envelope and caused quite a stir in the modest Viennese family where I was learning German. I couldn't imagine how the Ambassador's wife had come to hear of me or my address. The invitation put me into a spin. What did one wear on such an occasion? How did one behave? I hadn't the faintest idea even how to draft my acceptance. For, of course, the invitation must be accepted. I was seventeen and still had too little knowledge of the world to think of inventing a previous engagement.

The simple old Austrian sea captain and his wife had no more idea about these matters than I had. They had once, in early married life, been received at the Court of the Emperor Franz Josef. And for what it was worth to me they described the formality and splendour of that occasion.

'Things have changed now in Austria,' sighed the Captain, 'but no doubt in the British Embassy the old ceremonies are still kept up.'

In utter misery I pictured myself in my shabby tight-fitting grey suit, being led by haughty and resplendent footmen down glittering corridors and being ushered into some vast Salon where my appearance provoked a long audible titter down the line of assembled diplomats and courtiers.

In despair I had recourse to the only other Englishman I knew in Vienna, Kegwin. We had been at school together but as he was two years older than me had hardly known each other there. In Vienna we had met, on a more equal footing, a few times on the skating rink. Kegwin had already been a year in Vienna studying for the Diplomatic Service. He spoke German fluently, even the Viennese dialect, and represented in my eyes

the utmost that could be attained in sophistication and *savoir-faire*.

The next evening in the Graben Café, after two or three brandies for which I paid, I showed Kegwin the invitation.

'So glad they've asked you round,' he said, 'they are really such a charming couple.'

'Oh, you know them?' But of course Kegwin would know them. He knew everyone in Vienna.

'Very well. As a matter of fact I mentioned you were out here the last time I was there.'

So that was how they had heard about me. Humbly, I asked to be told the correct procedure to follow.

I must borrow, said Kegwin, a tail-coat from somewhere. I could wear my ordinary shirt and tie and even my grey flannel trousers. But a tail-coat was *de rigueur*.

'I would lend you mine,' he said, 'but I need it for a levee at the Swiss Legation.'

Then I must be sure to call both the Ambassador and his wife 'Your Excellency'. On arrival and on departure, and at least once during tea itself I must contrive to kiss the Ambassador's wife's finger-tips.

'But the finger *Tips* remember!' Kegwin repeated as we parted. 'That is strictly protocol.' And I thanked him almost with tears at the thought of the fool I might have made of myself without his advice.

The next morning, also on Kegwin's instructions, I delivered personally at the Embassy a note in my best handwriting addressed to 'Her Excellency, Wife of His Brittanic Majesty's Ambassador to the Austrian Republic.' The wording inside the note was on the same lines.

I must admit that I had doubts about the tail-coat which my captain dug out of an old trunk. It was dark green, with lots of brass buttons, epaulettes and various gold tassels. Even to my inexpert eye it seemed to clash with my yellow poplin shirt, flowery red tie and flannel trousers. However, the captain and his wife assured me that I looked 'herrlich' in it. It was the captain's frock coat or nothing and as Kegwin, who knew everything, had been so insistent on the point I felt I had better wear it.

I arrived by taxi at the British Embassy at 4.30 punctually. An English butler opened the door. I showed him my invitation card. He raised an eyebrow but without saying a word led me off down a dim corridor, knocked on a door, opened it and announced my name. I entered not a glittering Salon but merely a small sitting-room, very cosy and English looking, like the Ambassador and his wife themselves. They were seated at a tea table. There were no courtiers or diplomats present, only one other guest, a pretty English girl very smartly dressed, whom they called Susan.

If any of them were taken aback by my appearance they concealed it.

'I am so glad you could come,' said the Ambassador's wife holding out her hand.

'It was very kind of Your Excellency to ask me,' and as I spoke I bent low and kissed, with a loud sucking noise, the tips of her fingers.

'Won't you sit down?' she said, and I noticed her voice trembled a little.

I sat down. And it was then, as she poured me out some tea, that I saw my socks.

In those days you used to be able to buy socks at Woolworth's for sixpence a pair. They were made of a sort of pink string and quite shapeless. But they were economical, and I used to wear a pair for some weeks and then throw them away. I had brought several pairs with me to Vienna for daily use. I had intended to change them for this occasion but must, in the general excitement of getting dressed, have forgotten. Now sitting on the edge of my chair I caught sight of them, two pink string mufflers hanging round my ankles. I sat forward quickly and tried to make my trousers cover them. In vain. The trousers were too short.

I glanced up nervously and saw that the pretty girl Susan was staring at them too.

The next hour dragged. The Ambassador, his wife and Susan gossiped amusingly about art, people in Vienna, politics, life, literature, everything. They seemed to float effortlessly on a level

45

of intellectual brilliance that surpassed even Kegwin's. At first they made a polite effort to draw me into the conversation. I failed. 'No, Your Excellency,' 'Yes, Your Excellency,' was all seemed able to say. Thereafter I sat in silent misery trying to hide my feet under my chair and striving to think of something anything, which I could interpolate to show them that I was not really so dumb as I appeared.

But it was useless. I hardly understood a word of their talk. hadn't seen the pictures, read the books, listened to the music or even heard of the politicians they discussed so cleverly.

Once when my hostess offered me a second cup of tea I seized the opportunity of again kissing the TIPS of her fingers.

Then suddenly I saw my chance to shine.

They were on to Michael Arlen. The name rung a bell for me waited for a pause and then in a strained intellectual sort of voice spoke.

'Didn't you think he gave rather an interesting film perfor mance as Disraeli?'

There was silence. All eyes turned on me.

'Michael Arlen was in a *film*?' said the Ambassador's wife incredulously.

'I never knew he acted,' said the Ambassador.

For a moment I had their attention. I knew something after all that they didn't.

'Surely you've made a mistake,' said the pretty girl.

'No, no,' I insisted. 'He played Disraeli in the film about Queen Victoria. Of course, historically it wasn't accurate but I thought his interpretation. . . .' And then I saw too late how I had blundered. Oh, why hadn't I kept my mouth shut? Perhaps even yet no one would notice.

'How extraordinarily interesting,' said the Ambassador.

'How fascinating to know that,' said his wife.

'I think you are muddling him up with George Arliss,' said the pretty girl in a gentle voice barbed with malice.

Soon afterwards I took my leave, not forgetting to kiss the tips of the Ambassador's wife's fingers for the last time. What was that noise, I wondered afterwards, I had heard as the door shut behind me? A shrieking gurgling noise, that had sounded almost like wild hysterical laughter. But laughter in a British Embassy?

I didn't see Kegwin again in Vienna. He failed eventually in his examinations for the Diplomatic Service, and entered instead his family's canned-meat business. Where, so I heard later, he got shut by mistake in a refrigerator and was frozen to death. Very slowly, I hope.

Said the Earl to the Countess of Bective
" My dear, can it be the perspective
Or is your easterly tit
Just the least little bit
To the west — or my eyesight defective?"

" I Bach, he Offenbach, and dat is Debussy."

"Yes, Minister. But supposing the light at the
   end of the tunnel is really an oncoming train?"

"There's a dead fly in this tea!"
"I expect the hot water killed it."

A Walking Tour in Sardinia

Mrs Prendergast, the matronly bore against whom I had seemed for a long time to be irretrievably wedged, was telling me about her daughter Sabrina, a child-prodigy, as the daughters of matronly bores at parties so often are. This one evidently had already done everything that it might be possible for a seventeen-year-old girl to do and rather more. She had danced in the Sadler's Wells Ballet, had composed a string quartet which was to be played shortly on the Third Programme and had published a number of poems and children's books illustrated by herself.

I could almost feel my own inferiority complex expanding with the list of the girl's achievements. I wondered if perhaps I had had too many drinks.

'And what do you do, Mr Ah . . . hm . . . ?' asked Mrs Prendergast, politely suspending for the moment the subject of her daughter.

'Well . . . actually I try to paint.' It seemed hardly worth mentioning.

'And which do you paint, Mr Ah . . . hm . . . portraits or landscapes?'

The question, a familiar one, always brings out the worst in me.

'Neither, as a matter of fact,' I said, nonchalantly flipping my ash into her drink. 'Imaginary subjects more; sort of still life; I paint . . . I paint the foetus wallowing in its placental bog. . . .' I was sure now I had had too many drinks.

'Sounds fun . . .' murmured Mrs Prendergast. But we had been pinned together too long, her attention was wandering and I made my escape. A little later I met up with the fabulous daughter herself, who certainly appeared to be everything her mother had claimed, though surprisingly mature-looking for

seventeen. She was discussing with a friend the project of a holiday abroad in September.

'We want bathing and sun,' explained the friend, who then moved off.

'What have you planned so far?' I asked Sabrina.

'Well, we thought Sardinia might be a good bet in September but we can't find anyone who's ever been there to tell us.'

The opportunities of telling girls like Sabrina Prendergast my experiences in Sardinia are too rare. The good fortune must have shown itself in my face.

'Do *you* know Sardinia?' she cried. 'Why, that's wonderful. Let me just go and fetch Ursula. She'll be thrilled. Stay here, won't you? . . . Be back with her in a second.'

And while she fetched Ursula, I ran over the story in my mind.

It was quite a good story, really, if rather long and involved. The question was how, in telling it, to steer between the dangers of false heroics and of false modesty. And where to begin? In the plane perhaps, where I sat huddled in a coma of sheer funk, wondering how I should find the strength when the time came to move myself along the fuselage to that hole. The hole was decently covered with a detachable wooden lid. I kept peeping morbidly in its direction; and at the pale, drawn faces of my five companions, just visible in the dim red light.

Or later, the terror replaced by an almost joyful feeling of unreality and wonder, as we floated down on to the strange dead-coloured ground—like floating down on to the moon. We had hidden our 'chutes, £600 worth of pure silk, in the characteristic scrub or 'maquis', and I dare say the peasants of the neighbourhood are wearing silk shirts and pyjamas to this day. Then we

had crept off along the River Tirso, filling our water bottles from the muddy trickle, towards the German airfield a few miles to our north.

We knew absolutely nothing about the country we were in. Sardinia, I seemed to recall when briefed for the operation a few days before in Algiers, had usually changed hands in those confusing Treaties, following upon equally confusing Wars of Succession, that I had tried so unsuccessfully to learn about at school. Thereafter we had studied, hectically, air photographs and topographical surveys, but what can you really learn of a country from such things? The only features common throughout the island appeared to be the *nuraghe*—an extremely ancient form of conical stone hut; and the Sardinian peasant, who in his long black woollen cap and white stockings had determinedly resisted every outside influence for centuries and who, though not supposedly attached to his present Italian masters, must now be reckoned as potentially hostile to invasion by six British parachutists. Water, we had been assured—quite wrongly as it turned out—would be plentiful. For food, once our own tiny supply of dehydrated mutton and apricots had expired, we would have to live on the country. Did not the guide books say that at this time of year the fertile plains yielded rich crops of grapes, fruit, olives, corn, and so on?

But that was not a side to life in Sardinia that need concern Sabrina Prendergast and her friend. Perhaps they would be amused to hear how we had peered out of a thick bush at daybreak on our first morning in Sardinia and been able to identify, with delight, a *nuraghe* in the middle distance; and then, with less delight, a picturesque group of black-capped, white-hosed Sardinian peasants threshing corn in our immediate fore-ground. And how flocks of sheep and goats, with the menacing tinkle of their bells, had come nibbling at our bush and, with their attendant boy, had left us again still undetected.

Then there had been the episode round the airfield; the bush, chosen in the dark, which turned out in daylight to be beside the German guard tent; and the creeping about in the white dust of the airfield itself in search of planes we knew existed but could not find. And then the looking back, from the hardly reached hillside, as those planes we had been able to find went up suddenly with a blast that we felt a mile off, the blazing petrol tanks turning night into day and the exploding ammunition causing an altogether gratifying commotion all round.

In the weeks that followed we came to fear the insane mono-tonous and penetrating sound of sheepbells second only to the barking of dogs. In the wildest hills of Sardinia—and they are very wild—there is always a shepherd and his flock somewhere at hand. And often an old crone tending a patch of maize or beans outside the bounds, you would think, of all economic possi-bility. It was shepherds, shadowing us while the carabiniere were sent for, who caught us in the end on that last terrible night when, within a mile or two of our rendezvous with a submarine on the east coast, we were forced by thirst to leave the hills and search for water in the valley.

We had, by the time we were caught, explored a fairly representative cross-section of Sardinia on foot. Later, as prisoners, we visited one time and another by truck and rail, many of the towns in the north; Nuoro, Sassari, Alghero. . . .

Ending up in Maddalena, the port in the north-east corner, where we awaited an Italian destroyer to carry us across to Naples. On the eve of our departure two of us slipped past the sentry chatting to his girl, swam across the harbour and by an incredible piece of luck found a boat with oars and a sail. . . .

'Well, here we are,' said Sabrina Prendergast behind me suddenly.

'I hear you've been to Sardinia,' said her friend Ursula.

'I have been there, but not recently,' I said. 'As a matter of fact I walked across a lot of it once.'

'Oh, a walking tour! Not quite our cup of tea I'm afraid. We thought of going by train to Naples and from there you can apparently take a boat to a place called Maddalena where the bathing is said to be good.'

'Ah, Maddalena . . .' I murmured.

'Did you go there? Is the bathing *really* good?'

'As it happens,' I began slowly, hoping to create a certain air of mystery, 'almost exactly ten years ago to the minute, I was swimming off Maddalena. . . .'

But Miss Sabrina Prendergast, in the flush of successful youth, had no time for whatever middle-aged reminiscence was about to come.

'Was it *really* warm?' she interrupted me.

'Yes, it was beautifully warm, though it was in fact at night.'

'Ah, bathing at night, what heaven! Did you bathe naked?'

'It wasn't exactly a bathe and we were fully dressed. You see we . . .'

'We?' Their curiosity was delightfully aroused.

'Nothing very exciting I'm afraid in the way you mean. It was during the war and two of us were attempting . . .' But it had been a mistake to mention the War. Their faces fell.

'Oh, in the war . . .' they both said, making the War sound like some infinitely boring nineteenth-century Imperial episode.

'You were stationed there, I suppose,' said Sabrina Prendergast. 'Isn't that what you call it?'

Her mind, I could see, had conjured up a dreary picture of an English military camp at Maddalena and drunken officers plunging fully clad into the sea for a bet on a guest night.

I felt suddenly very old and dull and no longer disposed to tell them about Sardinia. Instead I recommended a book or two they might read on the subject and left. On the way out I became wedged for a moment again with Mrs Prendergast.

'Tell me, Mr Ah . . . hm . . .' she said, 'do you exhibit your feet or whatever it is you paint in the Academy?'

'Well, no, not actually.'

She gave me a quick look which seemed to say, 'the man's obviously a failure in his profession and so no good to me.'

'Of course, I suppose there is a lot of competition . . .' she murmured.

"Board of Trade?"
"who isn't?"

"And what does hors de combat mean?"
"Camp followers!"

Obliga Tories

Statu Tory

Ambula Tory

Von-statu Tory

Defama Tory

Preda Tory

Placa Tory

Goodbye Mr Gutz

Eheu fugaces . . . Twenty years ago this Christmas we shot *Mr Chips*.

It was a real white Christmas, the sort Mr Gutz, the Efficiency Expert from MGM, had dreamt about all his life in California, and the snow lay thick both inside the studios and out. Deep drifts all the way from the Dorchester to Denham, still deeper drifts—ARS GRATIA ARTIS—on the 15th century turrets and gables. In the Quad itself four hundred East End boys, dressed in toppers and Eton jackets, played merry hell with the tons of cotton wool. They came down daily in bus loads from Stepney—a few girls among them, we had reason to suspect.

Oodles of snow, too, on the Roll of Honour, though not so as to hide from the camera the names of F. Drake, W. Raleigh and H. Nelson. For it was a fine old school with tradition, and based, so far as the exigencies of the plot allowed, on Eton. I was some kind of assistant director, paid an extra ten bob a week for special technical knowledge—the only money I've ever managed to earn as the direct consequence of my education.

'Undo the bottom waistcoat button,' I used to bawl through a megaphone at the lads (and lasses?) from Stepney. 'And do up your flies.'

We technicians weren't affected, as a rule, by the subject matter of the films we shot. We looked, and felt, much the same among Welsh coal-miners, Chicago gangsters or Cornish smugglers. But on *Mr Chips* things were different, somehow. Partly it was Robert Donat, a greatly gifted, greatly beloved man, whose memory I salute with deep respect. His peformance was so convincing that, hard-boiled though we were, we really imagined ourselves back in an atmosphere of prefects and fags and Chapel and pi-jaws from the Head. Then the Art Department had excelled itself. Those fine old stones in the Quad, those fine old hammer beams in the Hall, infected every one of us with something of their lofty spirit, so that those who claimed fine old school ties pulled them boldly forth, to wear without shame. No wonder Mr Gutz softened up. Even Victor Savile, the Producer, became a fine old English gentleman—though he let the side down when we learnt, during the Munich crisis, that he had booked a passage to the States in the event of war.

The only trouble, in fact the occasion for Mr Gutz's presence among us, was the 'sked-ule'.

What with English incompetence, and not shooting at week-ends, and the fuss about getting details right, and actors muffing their lines, and Mr Donat's temperament (for it must be affectionately recalled that he had his moods) the film, which should have been done by Christmas, looked like extending into the New Year. And that suited most of us well enough. There were one and a half million unemployed in England at the time. The one million hung around places like Wigan and Ebbw Vale when they weren't blowing cornets in the Brompton Road and getting in the way of shoppers at Harrods. The half million hung around places like Wardour Street and Elstree and Denham. After *Mr Chips*, what? was the thought which occurred to many. Still, we had worked hard for three months and were pretty sore when Mr Gutz, under pressure from Hollywood, announced that shooting would continue for the whole of Christmas Day and Boxing Day. Even the fine old stones and hammer beams exuded disapproval. Only the kids from Stepney were delighted. They were having the time of their lives, and getting paid for it.

'I'm sorry, boys, but that's my jarb,' Mr Gutz said.

Before leaving Hollywood on this assignment he had been briefed by Mr Metro, Mr Goldwyn and Mr Mayer in person.

'See here Gutz,' they had told him, chewing at their cigars, 'You gotta put the heat on that limey unit. Wha-the-hell do they think they're playing at with our money? If they don't finish the jarb on sked-ule, buy some more that will. We gotta have *Chips* in the can by the Noo Year, to get it distributed before the real shooting starts over there. Chase that guy Savile, too. Make him sweat, Gutz. But go easy with Doughnut. He's barks arfis. . . .'

So, in mid-December, Mr Gutz had arrived, flourishing an iron studded flail like that terrifying picture by Low of Himmler descending on the Netherlands. He had the reputation of being a tough baby. And he was. Just that, really.

The temperature on the set, in spite of all the snow, was never below 100°, but he wore his teddy bear coat of palest fawn in all seasons. Beneath it a huge body tapered upwards into a long thick neck which, in turn, tapered without a noticeable break into a puffy little white face. The beady black eyes seemed less windows of a soul than two currants stuck, behind rimless spectacles, into an otherwise featureless duff pudding; you only saw he actually had a mouth when he smiled—because of the gold stoppings. He reminded me of some prehistoric herbivore—the Giant Sloth, was it?—doomed to extinction from lack of brain. But, brain or not, Mr Gutz was so damned *powerful* you had to take care not to be squashed.

Of course, to greet him, we had turned on every tap labelled 'charm'. That's what old school ties are best at, after all. A suite at the Dorchester—where the plumbing could be relied on; and a small part actor, with military moustache and bearing, to drive the Rolls. The Art Department fixed up the MGM motto in letters of gold a foot high outside the studio entrance. Mr Gutz had never actually noticed the motto before—it always gets sorta crowded out by that Lion.

'ARS GRATIA ARTIS', he read slowly aloud. 'Whazzat?' Sounds like some dirty crack.'

'It's Latin,' we explained. 'What they spoke in *Ben Hur* and *Quo Vadis?* times. It means Art for Art's sake.'

'Well, what d'ya know?' he said, and seemed pleased.

It was only the beginning, of course, but the seed had been sown. A few days afterwards when I took an Old Etonian tie to him in his office—he'd asked if he could wear one on the set—he said 'That motto—Arse what's it—what does it *really* signify, son?'

'Well Sir,' I said (calling him 'Sir' was part of the treatment, he loved it). 'It signifies that it doesn't matter how much money a film costs or how long it takes, so long as it's a good film. If I may

say this, Sir, I think *Mr Chips* is already a good film. Give us another month, and I believe it will be one of the really great films.'

By then we had his office full of chrysanthemums and holly wreaths and paper chains. The continuity girl had hung a bunch of mistletoe from the ceiling, though we felt that slightly overdid it—like H. Nelson on the Roll of Honour.

Mr Gutz stroked the whereabouts of his chin with a pachy-dermatous paw. I left him obviously *thinking*.

There were many signs, in the last three days before Christmas, of him unbending. He didn't actually break, how-ever, till late on Christmas Eve.

Partly, again, it was Robert Donat. At that point he was playing Mr Chips aged eighty-five and, by God, to see the frail old man holding his own among all those boys and in all that snow (we had the wind machine going and there was a blizzard) raised the same thought in every mind. 'You just *can't* ask him to act right on over Christmas without a break. He's a marvellous old boy, but you just can't *ask* it, Gutz.'

I was watching Mr Gutz closely and I think I saw a lump in his throat. When the four hundred Stepney boys began on the carols there were, unmistakably, two lumps. We'd turned off the wind machine and the lights. The whole set was lit by them holding candles. In the School Quadrangle . . . Up to their ars gratias in cotton wool . . . And a fresh dollop of sugar icing on the Roll of Honour . . . while they sang *Good King Wenceslas*—the cornier the better, for our purposes. Mr Gutz took out a handkerchief and blew the whereabouts of his nose.

That was the moment. The Producer, blowing his own nose, led him obsequiously into the Hall where the fur-trimmed scarlet outfit was in readiness. The Property man had been sent up to town to buy the largest and best. Also the sack of gifts. Catapults for the boys. And a few dolls for those that were really girls.

'A fine old English custom . . . Would you mind doing it, Sir? On behalf of Mr Metro, Mr Goldwyn and Mr Mayer?' Victor Savile asked. He was wearing a tweed cap and plus fours and an old Harrovian tie—at least such is my recollection.

Mr Gutz didn't mind. Indeed, he was greatly greatly moved. . . .

Later, the Property Man told me that Father Christmas's beard was soaked—but of course it may only have been sweat. Later again Mr Gutz gave me the telegram to send and I remember the wording exactly.

It was addressed to 'Metro, Goldwyn and Mayer, Holly-wood'. And the message read: 'We gotta great, repeat great, picture in the making here. Aim to finish shooting February, but not before. ARS GRATIA ARTIS. Signed GUTZ.'

Excellent Advice

Long, long ago, when I was leaving school, the master who had been trying to teach me German and French gave me two excellent bits of advice, which I now pass on to you.

The first was to memorise a few quotations in a foreign language. 'They'll come in handy one day,' said the wise and genial man. 'Even if you never find yourself in circumstances where you can quote them aptly, there will certainly be pauses in the conversation when a line or two of Italian, Portuguese or Scotch dropped into the silence may help to break the ice.'

Since then I have journeyed through life equipped with only two such quotations, both German and both learnt from him. I can't say I've often used them, and I can't at this minute check their accuracy, but near enough they are as follows.

Mit der Dummheit kämpfen Götter selbst vergegens.

That's from Schiller and means 'Against stupidity even the gods struggle in vain'. The other is a Goethe epigram:

Alles auf der Welt lässt sich ertragen
Nur nicht eine Reihe von schönen Tagen.

'Everything in the world is supportable except a row of fine days.'

Once, in the war, I quoted Schiller with some effect on a German sentry whom I needed to convince that I was a German officer. The Goethe, if unforgotten, has remained these thirty years in the junk room of my mind. Besides, living in England, it seemed such nonsense. How could one ever have a surfeit of fine weather?

Last month, in Tuscany, we had twenty-nine scorching, cloudless days on end and, though they were far from being insupportable, I did at least see what Goethe had perhaps meant. I even began to hope secretly for a shower, if only because Antonio's father grumbled that the grapes needed one and that

63

the wine would be ruined othewise. Watching him and his family work all day in the fields, I was thankful for a septic foot which provided an adequate excuse not to offer to help them. I was thankful, too, to be living in the comparative cool of a hill-top, wearing a shirt and shorts, rather than in Florence itself, which in this weather becomes an oven. And I cursed a great deal when, on the twenty-eighth day, I had to put on a suit and tie and shoes, and go to a formal lunch party which, in an unguarded moment, I'd accepted several weeks earlier.

The room was stifling, I knew no one else there, my shoes pinched, my suit and tie chafed, and I found myself seated between an empty chair, destined for another guest who wisely hadn't turned up, and an elderly German lady, of forbidding appearance and with a string of unpronounceable names and titles. From the awe with which she was treated I gathered she was something especially important, like a great-grand-daughter by marriage of the last Austrian Grand Duke of Tuscany, or something. On the whole I was glad that she ignored me and talked exclusively to the neighbour on her other side, an elderly and forbidding Italian gentleman who, I gathered, was also something especially important, like the cousin by marriage of the great-grandson of Queen Victoria, or something.

However, as the long, weary meal neared its close, the German lady turned and addressed a few gracious remarks to me. We conversed in English, since hers was much less rusty than my German; but I kept my two quotations in mind, should the opportunity arise.

As a rule, she said, nothing on earth would induce her to stay in Florence for August and September and, though her villa at Fiesole was cooler than most, she always went to the mountains. But this year, what with the expenses of her yacht and the iniquitous taxation and her losses at Monte Carlo, she had decided to economise and risk it. 'This would happen!' she explained, waving a hand to indicate the weather. 'I am always so unlucky.'

You have guessed? Yes, at a loss for anything else to say, I dug out my Goethe; at least, I intended to.

And this is where I should mention my old language master's second bit of advice; which was, for Heaven's sake not to get your quotations muddled. Because, as I realised some seconds too late, I had quoted the Schiller!

"Stop calling me 'Dad'!"

"I fed him with my own hands!"

"And here's one with a religious theme
which may appeal more to you, Bishop —
it's called 'Mary Magdalene'."

"And what do we learn from this beautiful story?"
"That you can't keep a good man down!"

By heaven, I've lost the keys

With all my strength I clung to my grandmother's ankles till they stopped kicking. Then I cut her down. . . . The opening sentence of an essay was the important thing, Mr Simpson told us. It needn't have too much, or even anything, to do with what followed but it must make the examiner sit up and say 'Gosh, this looks more like it.'

We sat up ourselves, that drowsy summer afternoon in 1927. Mr Mayhew, our usual form master, had gone ill with an appendix. Mr Simpson had been brought in from somewhere to finish preparing us for English and History 'O'-levels—or whatever the exam was called in those days.

Mouldy Mayhew was a straightforward sort of master who, like ourselves, regarded lessons as a tiresome necessity to be got through in order to enjoy the more important matter of games. He believed in hard work, in the memorisation of *facts*. So long as we learnt the answers to the questions we were likely to be asked, he didn't bother how we expressed them. Mr Simpson, we soon discovered, despised facts. He believed in ideas, in the use of language, in originality of thought. He was a cynical, melancholy fellow of about twenty-five, with staring dark eyes in a very pale face. He was said to have had a nervous breakdown, which was why the headmaster had been able to get him at short notice, but we never came to know him at all well and he left suddenly before the term ended.

'There's more to doing well in an exam than mugging up the subject like a parrot,' he continued, aware that he had our close attention. 'Any examiner sinks into a coma after fifty or sixty papers. I know, because I've been one for my sins. He can check the factual questions mechanically but it's the longer ones, the essay questions, that earn the real marks. The sort of essays you ll write will send him fast asleep. He'll simply give you a low average mark without bothering to wade through the sea of platitudes. A good opening sentence will at least wake him up. A strong image. Something with *punch*. Remember Bacon's 'What is truth? said jesting Pilate; and would not stay for an answer." If I were you I'd think up a few beforehand. With a little ingenuity you should be able to adapt them to almost any question. It will also help you to get started—that's half the battle in an essay. By the time you've finished writing the answer you may even decide to scrap the opening sentence and use it again—like the wooden centre of a brick arch.'

'Can you give us an example, sir?' asked someone.

'Easily,' said Mr Simpson—and he ad-libbed the thing about his grandmother's ankles. After that we called him Sinister Simpson.

I don't know about the others, but personally I took his tip and went into the exam armed with three or four ready-made openings—' "By heaven, I've lost the keys," said St Peter'; and so forth. But none had the same punch as Mr Simpson's line. I used it for a question on the causes of the French Revolution. When I'd finished, I found I could scratch it out, to use again for a question on Macbeth. As a matter of fact, I've often used it in the last forty years. I've used it now.

As for Mr Simpson, I never thought of him again till last week, at an Old Boys' Dinner in London. As a rule I don't go to them, because I hate seeing my contemporaries in an advanced state of physical decay and knowing that they're thinking the same about me. However, this one was in honour of Mouldy Mayhew himself and he'd written asking me to come—it didn't cheer me much to find that he now seemed the same age as the rest of us. He told us he had only missed one term at the school in fifty years—because of appendicitis—and someone said, 'Oh yes, I remember that. What was the name of that man who came in your place for a bit?' 'Simpson,' I said, pleased with the feat of memory. 'Sinister Simpson. He was a rather extraordinary chap. wonder what became of him.'

Mouldy Mayhew looked at me in surprise. 'Didn't you know?

It was hushed up, of course, but I imagined it had leaked out just the same.'

'No. What happened?'

'He was hung, poor devil. He murdered his grandmother.'

A serious-minded Rector, visiting his parishioners, got
no answer from one house. He left a card with a
quotation from The Revelation of St John 3.20. "Behold
I stand at the door and knock; if any man hear my
voice and open the door, I will come in to him."
The following Sunday a lady handed him her own card
with a quotation from Genesis 3.10. "I heard Thy
voice in the garden, and I was afraid, because
I was naked; and I hid myself."

A camel is a horse designed by a committee.

" I said ' Cecil says the great yob next to
you is the school bully ' ."

Some MUSICAL GAMES for Christmas Parties of ALL AGES & ALL NATIONS

Catch a Turian

Hump a dinck

Unravel

Seiza franc

Things Past in the Abruzzi

When the war cut short my promising career as a bottle-washer in the Film Industry, I vowed, as I shook the dust of Denham off my feet, never to return. Instead, when six years later I found myself free to choose, I took up Art. And it was then the problem began, which has grown ever since and which will so far as I can see continue to grow indefinitely. Namely, how to store the vast accumulation of little drawings which like most artists I feel impelled to make, usually on odd scraps of paper, of miscellaneous objects and sights which daily appeal to me.

At first a corner of the living-room floor accommodated the collection. Then a drawer. At present a large chest of drawers. Each year I make an effort to sort them out and reduce the number. Each year I fail. Often my wife tries to help. 'Surely,' she says, 'we can throw *that* away,' selecting the diagram of a Cornish pump-handle. 'Or that!', a weak, oh dear me how weak, study of a cat long since dead licking its tail. 'May come in useful sometime,' I mutter. And so the collection grows.

I seldom use the drawings. Nor even, except in the annual clear-out, look at them. But the memories which the sight of them periodically recalls are a real pleasure. They are there, part of my ever-lengthening past. To retain them lovingly is to some extent to defeat Time.

Recently a more than usually thorough overhaul brought to light, among a wad of shamingly inept juvenilia and some strange midnight aberrations, a batch of faded drawings of Italian peasant life in the Abruzzi; a hand-balance used for measuring corn; three bedraggled figures round a hearth; a shoemaker's last; some market scenes and others. I had forgotten their existence.

Attached to them was a typewritten letter from Allied Military Government, Rome, addressed to my wife: '. . . the enclosed were handed to our representative by Sinibaldo Amatangelo of the Abruzzi to be forwarded to you. We feel you would wish to know that he and his family are well and that he has been adequately compensated for his work in caring for your husband and his companions between September and December 1943. . . .'

With an overwhelming sense of Time regained the drawings carried me back nine years. Sights, smells and tastes long stored away now came rushing upon me with undiminished, even intensified clarity. And I thought again of Sinibaldo Amatangelo himself, that saintly wonderful man so aptly named.

After the Italian collapse in September 1943, two friends and myself, prisoners-of-war of the Italians, did what at that time and in those circumstances was the conventional thing to do and escaped. Many hundreds of others did the same. As most of them have since written books about their adventures, the story is a familiar, even, dare one say it, a monotonous one and I do not intend, except in the briefest fashion, to be guilty of retelling it.

For the first few days we were welcomed and entertained by many peasants. The Allies were expected to arrive in a matter of hours and we were handed round from one family to another as guests of honour. However, the Allies did not arrive. We were too weak from malaria to attempt the walk over the mountains towards them and our situation became serious. It was then that Sinibaldo Amatangelo, for no reason except that basic human kindness which the poor seem always to show to each other, took charge of us. And he was poor even for that neighbourhood. He possessed an acre of land scattered in inconvenient parcels over the hillside; a pig, a cow and some chickens. In a good year he and his family had just enough to eat. In a bad year they starved.

We lived in his hayloft at first, until the ever-widening depredations of the local German troops made that too risky; thereafter, for the next two and a half months, in a very small cave high up in the mountains, where Sinibaldo visited us every three days with food. In fine weather the journey up and back took him five hours. In the snow—and for the last six weeks there was heavy

75

Supper with Sinibaldo.

snow—it must have been nearer eight hours. I have often wondered whether, if our situations were reversed and Sinibaldo was hiding-up in, let us say, one of the caves round Churt, I should have the inclination to carry food across to him twice a week from Farnham, Surrey.

On one occasion, in a snowstorm, he carried up as well as food, an iron shoemaker's last, with which as we huddled towards the back of the cave out of the driving snow, he repaired our tattered boots.

Quite apart from the time and effort involved, the feeding of three extra people for so long must have placed an intolerable strain on his resources. But he did it almost joyfully and at the time we were in too desperate a state to ask ourselves how he could do it.

Hunger, in spite of Sinibaldo's generosity, was our chief enemy, and after hunger, boredom. When I could, I drew. But paper was scarce and, as it was, many of my drawings came to an ignoble end. The most memorable of them was a huge nude, done not on paper but with a stick of burnt wood on a suggestive surface of the cave wall. I like to think of it puzzling archaeologists of the future; a minor, very minor, Altamira in the Abruzzi.

By mid-December life in the cave had become insupportable. There was no sign that the Allies would arrive before the spring and malaria or no malaria we decided to set off over the mountains. We descended to Sinibaldo to collect supplies and to spend a last comfortable night on his hay. He tried to persuade us to stay on with him through the winter, despite the appalling risks to himself. Then, seeing we were determined, he begged us to let him come with us. But we refused. He had already done too much, far too much. Our future lay with ourselves alone. So he climbed with us for the first few hours and we said goodbye at last in the moonlight. He was crying like a child as he kissed each of us in turn on both cheeks. And he was still standing there looking after us when we turned several times to look back. Until at length the shadowy figure and the pale blob on top of it slowly evaporated into the night.

Perhaps I should confess that not all the drawings reproduced here are those that Sinibaldo eventually returned through Allied Military Government. I revisited him one day in August, 1947, nearly four years after these events. The visit was a sad fiasco. The welcome, the hospitality were overwhelming, merciless. So was the August sun. I had, when I arrived, a severe headache from the heat. To avoid offence meal after meal had to be eaten with Sinibaldo and his neighbours, about six heavy peasant meals together, between midday and midnight! And that rough home-made wine which had seemed so wonderful in 1943 was now, virtually, poison which, because of the sentiment of the occasion, I could not refuse. My headache was joined by a hangover and what should have been the most moving reunion of a lifetime became almost unendurable misery.

That night I slept not on Sinibaldo's delicious hay but in his best bed. I was eaten alive.

In the morning I insisted that I had with great regret to be back in Rome and I hated myself for being so thankful to see the small mountain train arrive at the station. As, in how different a mood,

I kissed him again good-bye, I promised to return in a year or two.

Sinibaldo shook his head sadly. 'I do not think you will ever come back again,' he said. 'What is there for you in a place like this? We only stay here because we have no money to leave.'

And as I waved to him from the carriage window I knew he was right. I felt very small.

I said at the beginning that I had vowed never to return to the Film Business. It was not a vow I've ever had much inclination to break, except once. Some years after the war I heard in a roundabout way that the company I had worked for were searching for a script about escaped POW in Italy. I had written an elaborate and no doubt much dramatised account of my own adventures after they occurred. Hopefully, I sent this to an acquaintance with whom in the old days I had washed bottles, so to speak, shoulder to shoulder and who was now a producer. (If only I'd kept on at it where might I not be now?) After a year I had a reply. 'We think your script is fine, fine,' he wrote, 'just what we have been looking for and we should like to buy it.' He mentioned a fabulous sum. 'There are just some slight alterations we shall need you to make first. To give dramatic interest, you know. We would like your two companions to be, one a reformed American gangster, the other a Russian polit-buro agent. And to give sex-interest, the part of Sinibaldo Amat-angelo must be changed into an ex-Fascist blonde.'

I had a moment of weakness. I think it was the memory of the shoemaker's last which tipped the balance. 'For money, enough money, I will gladly change two eminent Guards officers into anything you like to name,' I wrote back. 'But Sinibaldo Amat-angelo stays as Sinibaldo Amatangelo and that's final.'

I didn't hear again from the Film Company. Perhaps if I had accepted their offer, I should not now have been reduced to writing for the papers.

"The wuns with teethmarks have hard centres."

"And who was it who killed Jesus Christ?"
"Judas asparagus!"

COMMON MARKET NEWS

The Lord's Prayer contains 70 words;
The Apostles Creed 111;
The Ten Commandments 297;
The American Declaration of Independence 300;
The European Economic Community Directive
on the Export of Duck Eggs 26,911.

"My name is Fifi. F-I-F-I."
"My name is Mimi. M-I-M-I."
"And mine is Fido. P-H-Y-D-E-A-U."

Why did they cut off poor John the Baptist's head?"
Because Salami danced naked in front of Harrods."

Mr Ching

More reliable than mescalin, less chancy than phenobarbitone, as an effective dispeller of *Angst* he can have had few equals since Perseus freed Andromeda. In our immediate family circle his wizardry—for such it was—increased the birth rate sixfold in as many years. And I only heard of him by chance at a London party soon after the War. With two old friends, an actress and a sculptor, I had retreated from the surrounding din to a quiet corner and happened to mention my worry.

'But don't you claim expenses—the cost of paint and canvases, visits to galleries and publishers and so forth?' she asked.

'No. Should I?'

'Of course, you ass,' the sculptor said. 'I'm allowed a third of the rent and two thirds of the telephone. What about the hire of models?'

'I wouldn't know what to do with a model even if I could find one in outer Suffolk'—my pictures were based on abstract carpet patterns at the time.

'Nor frankly would I'—he constructed curious objects with pink string and sealing wax. 'But models are a legitimate expense. I hire £500 worth on my return. They're always armed with cornucopias. I live largely on pineapples and grapes—thanks to Mr Ching.'

'So you're a Ching-ite too!' the actress cried. 'He's a genius. I just post him all my figures and he jiggles them around and adds a few more and then sends them off with a long covering letter. It's the most heavenly gibberish, like *Finnegan's Wake*.'

'The letters are indeed quite brilliantly obscure,' the sculptor agreed. 'No wonder they tie the tax people up in knots.'

Neither of them had ever met him. Apparently he preferred to deal with clients by post and telephone, conducting his crusade on their behalf from a furnished room in West Ealing.

'I do hope he gets a vicarious kick out of it all somewhere,' the actress said. 'La Vie de Bohème at second hand. . . . His own life must be deadly.'

Not that I had much reason to complain. A wife, a child, an oast house, my own master. . . . The beard and corduroys alone, symbols of recent emancipation from the service of the King, more than made up for grinding poverty. The trouble really was that the gentlemanly torpor of army life had unfitted me for the terrors of civvy street. Against Inspectors of Cavalry, red in face and hat, I could defend myself. Against Inspectors of Taxes, red in tooth and claw, I was helpless. In the joyous early days of peace I kept afloat with teaching and a knack for drawing funny faces. The hard-won cheques were scrupulously listed. In April, with naïve pride, I declared their total on the buff form. When in June another form, a white one, bluntly demanded back again a sum which by then bore only the most whimsical relation to my bank balance, the whole thing came as a bitter shock.

In desperation, therefore, I rang Mr Ching long-distance, determined to meet him personally before committing myself. Lacking refinement in such an approach I shouted more aggressively than ever through my beard. It must be confessed too that the King's Service had roughened my speech.

'Those old crooks X and Y put me on to you,' I said, after crudely giving my name and business. 'They tell me you're a marvel at diddling the bloody sharks in the taxation office.'

'Oh yes . . . ?' In the long distance the prim little voice sounded icily discreet. Perhaps it wasn't done to mention clients on the phone? And then 'I don't know that the expression . . . er . . . diddle is quite how I would prefer to describe my professional activity, but I think I may flatter myself that I am sometimes able, from long experience in these matters, to render assistance in the case of a self-employed individual engaged in one of the . . . er . . . artistic fields.'

We need not confer in person, he thought, if I would send particulars. After three lots of pips, I nailed him down to a morning when we should both be in the Piccadilly neighbourhood. On the spur of the moment and with a fourth lot of pips coming up, I invited him to lunch at the Ritz.

'In case there are other beards and corduroys about, I'll be leading a lobster on a string.'

No smile came back over the wire. 'Oh I shouldn't trouble to do that, Mr Bunthorpe. You'll recognise me easily I'm sure. I'm eighty years old and very short for my age.'

So, all that time ago now, I sat in the Ritz lounge, glaring with contempt at the other customers and unobtrusively checking the money in my wallet. Then I ordered two martinis.

I recognised him at once. Not especially *Chinese*, but a diminutive sprightly figure with a face like a withered autumn leaf, neat and sharp as a black pin in dress, and carrying a huge briefcase. There were, as it happened, no other beards and corduroys and he recognised me too.

'I find it hard to believe you can be eighty, Mr Ching.' (He might in fact have been any age between sixty and a hundred.)

He answered with a little smirk and a bow, his look plainly saying 'Let's have no hollow compliments, *please*.'

'A cigarette before lunch?'

'Very kind, but . . . thank you, no. I never indulge . . .'

'A martini then?'

'Very kind, but I'm afraid . . .' He gave a vaguely gastric gesture.

I drank them quickly myself, hoping he didn't notice how little change was returned from a pound note. But seated on the chair's edge, nursing the briefcase on his knee, he noticed everything, his expression reminding me of a certain octogenarian philosopher—an expression of intense curiosity despite intense disillusion.

'Well then, let's go on in and have a damn good lunch,' I said in my hearty ex-military way.

But he cared no more for food than for alcohol and tobacco and with the waiter's caustic eye on us, ordered simply a small helping of boiled rice. More amply provided I broached my business.

'This is the general picture. . . .' The outline of my domestic
set-up and earnings didn't take long.

'Of course, you may not feel able to help me at all. . . .'

'We shall see, we shall see. Have you nothing written down,
no list of receipts, no accounts?'

'I'm afraid I've never kept accounts.' It was like admitting to a
bishop that I'd never been to church. But evidently Mr Ching
was quite accustomed to laxity of the sort; as, doubtless, bishops
also are.

'Receipts are not absolutely *essential*, though they do help.
Artists can be so very . . . inconsequential. . . . But it is difficult
for them, I do see that. And I try to make the HMI see it too. I
always tell him he can't expect to differentiate between private
life and business in the case of artists and other self-employed
individuals. He must be prepared to assess their home and their

work as a *whole* and once I've got him to realise that, he usually agrees to my figures. It's just a question of getting him to, er, *realise*. . . . HMI's are quite reasonable, you know, as a rule. I think you were perhaps just a little *too* severe the other day on the telephone. . . .'

'Yes, I'm sorry about that, Mr Ching. I'm afraid my language hasn't recovered yet from . . . from the rough male kiss of army blankets . . . the War, and all that.'

'Ah yes, the War. A very tiresome time. We had a bomb in West Ealing. But there's just one other matter. You must please understand that I am only concerned with helping you claim those items of expenditure which, as an artist, you can quite legitimately claim for professional expenses. You mentioned the word—er—*diddle*, I believe. There's no question of that you know, no question.'

He pulled out a typewritten sheet. 'Here is a suggested list of the items; not exhaustive, but I find it useful as a guide. Could we just run through it, to give you the idea? You might care to fill the details in more exactly at your leisure.'

The first part of the list covered basic costs like rent, heating and telephone and he jotted down my estimates. But it was the second part, those items of particular relevance to a painter, which truly reflected the extent of Mr Ching's ingenuity.

'Excursions undertaken with the object of gaining inspirational matter; entertainment incurred in connection with the sale, or contemplated sale, of work; acquisition of property for use in the studio; visits to theatres, exhibitions, etc., with the purpose of keeping in touch with current trends;' and dozens more. The headings were so elastic it was hard to think of a single expense which mightn't be included under one or other of them.

'About the only thing you don't mention is food!'

'Ah, I'm afraid food cannot be claimed as such.' He paused and added, 'Except, of course, where it has to be expressly obtained for purposes of Art. To feed your models, for instance; or to use in a picture. You paint Still Lives a great deal, I expect?'

'Well as it happens I have a garden and actually my paintings . . .' But I caught his quizzical glance. 'That is, yes, of course, I do paint quite a lot of Still Lives.'

'Still Lives with meat occasionally . . . ?'

'Oh yes, often with meat. And fish. I'm very fond of painting fish; and lobsters. Oysters too. . . .'

'Good,' he said, 'good.' And rubbed his hands. There was—but I could not be sure—the hint of a twinkle in his eye. At his next question there was—but again I could not be *quite* sure—a glint of lust.

'Do you paint much—from the Life, as I believe it is known?'

Go on, give the old boy his vicarious kick, I thought.

'Certainly, a great deal. And they all eat like horses afterwards.'

By the time we'd finished we calculated that the Inland Revenue Department owed me hundreds and hundreds of pounds.

'Do you really think there's a chance of getting any of it back?' I asked, feeling slightly giddy.

'Oh yes, I think we'll get it back all right, or most of it. But I'm afraid I must be moving on to my next appointment. Let me have the final figures as soon as you can.'

The waiter brought the receipted bill and my change on a plate. In a lordly fashion I waved him to keep it. But Mr Ching quickly popped the bill into his briefcase. It was the only time he actually smiled.

'I'll take charge of this for you.'

We parted under the Ritz arcade.

'Thank you, Mr Bunthorpe. That was quite an unusual little treat for me,' he said.

'For me, too, Mr Ching. I think you're bloody marvellous.'

'Oh, I wouldn't go so far as that.' He spoke without the slightest trace of boastfulness. 'I just like to think of myself sometimes . . . as the . . . champion of the self-employed.'

And with jaunty little steps he strode off down Piccadilly.

I wish I still had my copy of the first of the countless letters Mr Ching wrote to the HMI. He did his own typing and the long sentences, crammed with spelling mistakes and misprints, wound on and on down the pages, losing themselves in a bog of sums, references to Clauses and Sub-Sections of Ministerial Directives, and such like. Thanks to them, in part also to my preparation of the basic raw material on which Mr Ching went to work, the HMI came before too long, and with an almost audible sigh of defeat, to *realise*. . . .

Freed from *Angst*, my home life and profession flourished, and were agreed by the HMI to flourish, as a *whole*. I and my wife and, in increasing number, children enjoyed many holidays abroad undertaken with the object of gaining inspirational matter. A station waggon was purchased and maintained towards the sale, or contemplated sale, of pictures whose subject, however obliquely, remained firmly based on haunches of venison, lobsters, oysters. . . . To the same legitimate end thousands of corks were drawn from bottles for the professional entertainment of Art Critics and Gallery Dealers. And once the memory of serving the King had sufficiently receded I shaved off the beard, charged the green corduroys against Capital Depreciation and acquired a dark double-breasted city suit as a property for use in the studio.

Nor—let it be recorded to my credit—while I throve and multiplied, was I forgetful of Mr Ching, all alone there in his furnished room. Never a Christmas passed but a pineapple, a salmon, or whatever else might be spared from feeding my models, would be delivered in a battered mess at his door by the postal authorities of West Ealing.

Mr Ching and I did not meet again. But we exchanged many sheets of words in April of each year, spent many hours all told conversing, as he would put it, on the telephone—the HMI having accepted a figure of 99 per cent of the telephone bill for professional use. Occasionally he would ring me, to suggest the reconsideration of some item tenuously claimed.

'The HMI is querying the box of orchids in cellophane, delivered at the stage door of the Gaiety, as a legitimate studio property,' he said to me only last month. 'I was going to rearrange the figures, with your approval, so as to include it under expenditure on publicity.'

In fact, my friend the actress had bought one of my paintings in a mixed exhibition and the flowers were partly a little *quid pro quo*, partly just a gesture for old time's sake which might lead, who could tell, to her buying another picture if her own show went on running. Either way it was money well spent, and, I strongly felt, a perfectly legitimate expense. By happy chance my large abstract *Symphony in Mauve* had just been accepted by the Academy for their modern room. The Secretary, I knew, would agree to my changing the title in the catalogue at the last minute—not for nothing had I given him and his wife dinner at Claridges.

'Tell the HMI,' I said glibly, 'that I'm sending him an invitation to this year's Royal Academy Private View where, if he takes the trouble to look, he will find my picture *Orchids under Cellophane* hung on the line. If it sells, he'll be getting 75 odd quid out of me. And all I'm claiming is a miserable £10 for the raw materials.'

'Well that's fairly convincing,' Mr Ching said. 'Except that "Delivering at the stage door of the Gaiety" is written on the bill.'

'Of course it is. I couldn't reach the shop before they shut and got them to send the flowers to the theatre where I had to meet the Producer. There's some talk of my doing a décor. . . .'

'Good,' Mr Ching said. 'He can't say much to that. It's conclusive.' He paused; and I could have sworn he chuckled softly. 'You have come a long way since the very pleasant occasion of our meeting.'

'I often think of it, too, Mr Ching. How are you keeping?'

'Oh, as well as can be expected at my age. Very busy, you know, at this time of the year. You and your family are well, I hope?'

'Oh yes, we're all right. The floods have gone down a bit so we can use the kitchen—I'll be putting in a claim for that later. I'm afraid I can't hear you clearly. The children are making the hell of a racket.'

'Ah yes, children.' The long distance voice sounded very faint. 'They can be troublesome, so I'm told. But I think you're lucky to have them all the same, you know. I think you're lucky. I—I am very much alone.'

We were cut off. It was the last time we spoke. Appropriately the cheap black-edged envelope arrived by the same post as the Demand from the Inland Revenue Department. I was puzzled by the envelope, recognising Mr Ching's typewriter. For whom was he in mourning? I opened the other quickly first and noted, with satisfaction, the Nil Assessment. Well done, Mr Ching. Then I opened his. It contained simply a sheet of his notepaper, and on it a message printed, unmistakably, by himself. 'Mr Ching has asked me to notify his clients in the contingency of his passing unexpectedly on, which sad event, I regret to inform you, has now occurred. The funeral will take place at ———.' The details had been added in handwriting by his landlady, who signed the letter. Methodical to the last, he must have prepared all the envelopes himself and given them to her to post 'in the event . . .'

I felt the loss as more than a mere loss of income—considerable though that would now be—and motored over in the station waggon all the way from Suffolk to the funeral in West Ealing. It was the usual melancholy affair, with the landlady and myself the only mourners. But the flowers were beautiful, about a hundred contributions. Among them my own, I was glad to see, were the most magnificent. 'To Mr Ching, Champion of the Self-Employed, with deep admiration and gratitude' I had inscribed on the card. The other tributes bore similar messages.

That night, when I returned home, I sat long at my desk sucking my pen and staring at the account book in which nowadays I enter everything before I forget. 'To the purchase of floral material and other expenses incurred in connection with Still Life Object £35,' I wrote. Then I scratched that out and made it £55.

I think he would have been pleased.

'——Ah, sketching, I see, what fun . . .'

Dappled things

'Glory be to God for dappled things—for skies of couple-colour as a brinded cow. . . .' So far as I'm aware, Gerard Manley Hopkins never saw the Florentine church of St Maria Novella, but he would surely have loved it—as I am loving it, from the shade of a little restaurant after lunch. (Glory be, also, to *Trippa alla Florentine*, i.e. Florentine tripe.) Santa Maria Novella is one of the world's masterpieces of dappling, of couple-colouration and of brindedness, its outside being entirely covered with the skins of a thousand marble zebras, arranged in bands, lozenges, circles and squares.

In my present somewhat irreverent after-luncheon mood, it occurs to me that I would like St Maria even more if the whole thing was an elaborate fake, a masterpiece not of marble but of *marbling*. Since it was my own enthusiasm for marbling that resulted in the hasty decision to leave England, I may as well sit here in the cool an hour longer, telling you about that enthusiasm while I finish the Chianti, instead of risking my life in the baked streets to visit the Uffizi (pronounced oof-it's he).

Enthusiasm did I say? Call it, rather, a passion, a disease, a vice almost. I hope I may succeed in infecting some of you.

What started me off (or us off, for my elder children soon caught the bug) was *Three Methods of Marbling*, a little pamphlet published by Dryad Handicrafts for 1s.

To marble *expertly* you need years of experience, oodles of patience and a sort of glue called Carrageen moss which I've never troubled to find and is anyway virtually unobtainable. To marble as *we* did, you need, beyond a slapdash love of experimenting, some sort of tray, a packet of size (cold-water paste and glue are OK), a few oilpaints, a bottle of turps-substitute, and masses of cheap slightly-absorbent white paper or card.

Mix the size with water to the consistency of thin milk and fill e tray. Dilute two or three oil colours with turps to the same onsistency—we used cardboard cups from Woolworth's—and rinkle them on to the surface; the size helps to keep the colours parate. 'Comb' the colours together with a twig, feather, or en a comb. Take your paper (which, to handle easily, should e slightly smaller than the tray) and, greatly daring, lay it flat on e surface for a few seconds. Then lift it smartly off again, turn it ce up on the floor to dry—and there, more or less, you are. Too ick a mixture of paint produces a messy, if magnificent, *chiste*-type picture—in which case, try taking a second impresson with another sheet of paper. Too thin a mixture yields only a intly brinded result. But you will quickly evolve your own ethod.

That is just the *start* of the marbling disease; a period of gaining onfidence, the stage when you're still content with a smallish ay and sheets of foolscap. Some of *our* best effects were chieved on the original designs for past *Elizabethan* covers. We ad a craze for marbling all notepaper and envelopes—to obtain blank area you simply damp part of the paper with a brush efore dipping; the damp part 'resists' the oil paint. (The techique offers infinite possibilities. My eldest daughter used to rush in the shape of a horse on envelopes, writing the address on e body, sticking the stamp on the head.)

But as our skill increased, so did our ambition. We longed to ork big, and still bigger. To get a larger printing surface we oved from tray to sink, from sink to bath. (It's less unhygienic an it sounds. The paper lifts most of the paint off the water— nly a little clings to the sides of the bath and that, *so long as it is ot allowed to dry*, can be wiped off easily.) We stitched marble aper into lampshades, we marbled existing lampshades, rolling em slowly over the oily surface. Almost every piece of paper or aterial of a single light colour seemed to us, in our mania, to cry ut for embellishment. We tore down a wooden fireplace, gave e component parts a coat of matt white paint before dipping em, and lo!—we had a new marble fireplace, or we would have ad, if we could have been bothered to put it all back.

Our ambition continued to grow. We dreamt of marbling the

whole of our house, to make it a sort of Byzantine palace. I bought a vast roll of lining paper, but the bath was too short and narrow. Besides, we intended to marble all our doors as well. We unhinged and dehandled several and stood them against the jambs, in readiness. But what hope was there of ever finding a bath large enough? We began to feel desperately frustrated, our talent hemmed-in and stifled. And then we saw the tank arrive on the transporter.

Not an Army sort of tank. A gigantic glassfibre container; a ready made swimming pool. A crane followed and unloaded the tank into the garden of our neighbour, into the hole that we had occasionally watched him digging all winter.

A shy bachelor, he had only come to live next door the previous autumn. We hardly knew him. Now, when we could see that the swimming pool was finished, we invited him round.

'Did you say you'd been here some time?' he asked, incredulously, glancing at the dismantled fireplace, the door propped against the doorpost, the samples of marbled paper littering the floor or sticky taped on the walls.

'Oh, for years,' we said.

He glanced, more nervously still, at a large sheet of paper, the exact size of our bath, that my son had pinned up over the fireplace. (As a piece of marbling it had been a failure. As an apocalyptic vision it had something—or so my son claimed.)

'I'm afraid I don't understand modern art, if that is modern art,' said our neighbour.

'Do a lot of bathing?' I asked, to lead the conversation round to where we wanted it. And so, after a drink or two, he unbent and told us about the pool.

Swimming pools were evidently his passion in life, what marbling, just then, was to us. He had spent all his savings on this one, which he had made to his own design. You could fill it, he said, through a special high-pressure tap in fifteen minutes, and empty it, through a special high-pressure plug hole, in ten. The bottom and sides were painted to a pattern and with a turquoise green of his invention. In it you had the impression of being in the Blue Lagoon in Capri.

'I've patented it under the name *The Pocket Lagoon*,' he added.

'How big is it?' asked my son. I knew what was in his mind.

'Oh, not very large. Twenty-three nine by eleven ten and a half.'

I made a swift mental calculation. 'Nearly sixteen times the size of that door,' I said, and my son and daughter both whistled. They knew what was in my mind.

'Yes, about that, I suppose.' I refilled his glass, wondering how to approach the next step. But there was no need.

'Look,' he said. 'I've got to go off tomorrow for a week. Business conference up north. But the pool's there, all filled and ready. You can go across and use it anytime you like.'

'That's awfully decent of you, sir,' said my son.

'Oh, but I don't think they should, when you're not there,' said my wife. 'I mean, they might damage it.'

'Nothing to damage. Foolproof. An elephant couldn't do any harm. All I ask is, don't fiddle with any of the knobs. You'll see them on the side. The re-chlorinating plant, intake-valves and so on. I'll enjoy thinking of all your fun.'

We agreed, that evening, to keep the colour scheme very simple. A faint undertone of brick red, strongly overlaid with pure black. The next morning we rushed out and bought five gallons of the hardest and fastest-drying enamel paint, twenty gallons of turps-substitute, and four long-handled dusters for combing. We decided not to use size, hoping that the chlorine in the water would serve the same purpose, which it seemed to.

In the first three days, working flat out, we marbled six doors (both sides), and about two hundred and fifty yards of paper, two feet six inches wide. Technically, we were at the top of our form. Sheet after sheet came off, each more lovely than the last. We were scrupulous, too, about cleaning up.

Disaster struck on the fourth day. We had flooded a fresh lot of paint on when my wife called us in for lunch. I maintain that my son must have twiddled a knob—he is an inveterate twiddler. He swears he did not and that I must have stumbled against a valve, lifting a door out. However it happened, when we returned to work only forty minutes later, the pool was empty. Every drop of water had drained. The turquoise green lining was hidden beneath a skin—an *irremovable* skin—of red and black. A masterpiece of dappling in its way; Gerard Manley Hopkins would have appreciated it. But would our neighbour?

We didn't wait to find out.

" Thank you for sending me a copy of your book. I shall waste no time in reading it...